BOOK ABT FANTASY

BOOK ABT FANTASY

BY CHRIS SYLVESTER

ROOF BOOKS
NEW YORK

ISBN: 978-1-931824-68-2
Library of Congress Control Number: 2016956278

Cover art by metal sculptor Ricardo Breceda,
Anza–Borrego Desert State Park, CA

 This book is made possible, in part, by the New York
State Council on the Arts with the support of
Governor Andrew Cuomo and the New York State Legislature.

Roof Books are distributed by
Small Press Distribution
1341 Seventh Street
Berkeley, CA. 94710-1403
Phone orders: 800-869-7553
www.spdbooks.org

Roof Books are published by
Segue Foundation
300 Bowery
New York, NY 10012
seguefoundation.com

CONTENTS

BOOK ABT FANTASY BY CHRIS
SYLVESTER PART ONE: 14 PT.
FONT

poems abt arrangement demonstration and fantasy with one still life that happens after it by chris sylvester

1/ demonstration like show 'it' like demonstrating and making everyone disappear even beyond satisfaction i.e. my satisfaction i.e. gloves plant left and right hands paintballs camera syringes 'it'

2/ demonstration as maybe a 'compact space' partially organizing regulating or whatever at least overlaid with descriptions i.e. 'tell' you about the jet ski and 'tell' you about the jet ski and 'tell' you about the jet ski to like 'show' or pretend to 'show' you the jet ski to be 'shown' or pretend you are 'shown' the jet ski so as to 'make' both of us and the jet ski and everyone else 'disappear'

3/ so there is an arrangement and of course whatever the arrangement is a demonstration and of course it is also a fantasy about demonstration and so there is something about an arrangement and how it is a demonstration of fantasy and also a fantasy of demonstration and maybe there is somewhere like a question about satisfaction or enjoyment or maybe it is not actually a question but it is almost like a question and it has to do with some kind of point in a given demonstration that has to do with fantasy or whatever and it also has to do with a point in whatever fantasy that is pretty much a demonstration basically if it was actually a question it would have to do

with enjoyment or satisfaction and it would

have everything to do with also being

somewhere else

4/ given that something is said i guess about 'it' and that saying something about 'it' is probably like a demonstration of 'it' or somehow a showing of 'it' as maybe an arrangement and given that 'needing one's help' or 'helping one find it' is also kind of like a demonstration or whatever and given all of that there is something maybe about how 'i' want to be a weak or little thing or something about how 'i' want to be a weak and tiny thing that maybe gets to be lodged somewhere in 'you' like really 'in there' like in 'you' where 'i' am still only a little thing and i am still only a tiny thing and 'i' am still only a weak thing but 'i' also get like a non-demonstrable big-ness or large-ness

somehow which is like a swimming pool or

over-sized hot tub that is always behind 'you'

or over your shoulder and that 'you' cannot

see but that 'you' feel 'you' might be able to

demonstrate might possibly be able to

demonstrate

5/ so that if/when the fantasy fades given that it will fade and at the very place where it does given that the fantasy does not fade all at once there will have always been something there at that place like a thomas kinkade painting or a magic eye poster or a whatever ophthalmologist's waiting room and given that this 'will have always been' is formal or may be given in a formal sense so that the light or the 3d form of a blue whale or the earth-toned carpet and chairs will no more be encountered in the fading than you or i or the fantasy itself and/or maybe there will only ever have been that moment when the criminal realizes that he has been swallowed in 'black giantess police 2' but

does not cry only holds his arms and hands

up like what or what is a stomach

still life:

a smoking field

a smoking field and ash and sod

and a giant mechanoid form too beautiful to describe

moving off to the north when the sun breaks through the miasma

and glinting off its various parts

and there are no humans

THE MACROPHILIA POEMS BY CHRIS SYLVESTER

MACROPHILIA POEM #1

I AM BIG

I AM A BIG THING OR CREATURE

I AM VERY BIG

I WILL STEP ON YOU BUT I WILL NOT CRUSH YOU

I WILL ONLY STEP ON YOU

MACROPHILIA POEM #2

I AM BIG

I AM SO BIG

I CAN PUT YOU IN MY MOUTH

I CAN PUT YOU IN MY MOUTH AND KEEP
YOU THERE OR I CAN SWALLOW YOU

AND I CAN SAY THINGS EITHER AROUND
YOU LIKE SAYING THINGS WITH MY BIG
MOUTH FULL OR AFTER I HAVE
SWALLOWED YOU

I CAN SAY THINGS LIKE 'WELCOME TO
YOUR NEW HOME' OR 'YOUR LITTLE
BODY IT TASTES SO GOOD' OR
'DOWN YOU GO' OR 'MAKE YOURSELF
COMFORTABLE'

MACROPHILIA POEM #3

I AM BIG I AM SO BIG

AND WHEN YOU SEE ME YOU WILL NOT
BE ABLE TO SEE ME ALL AT ONCE

YOU WILL ONLY BE ABLE TO SEE ME
PIECE BY PIECE

AND EACH PIECE WILL ALSO BE SO BIG

MACROPHILIA POEM #4

I AM SO BIG

I DO NOT CARE WHAT YOU WANT

I DO NOT CARE WHAT PEOPLE WHO
ARE YOUR SIZE WANT

I ONLY CARE ABOUT WHAT I WANT

WHAT I WANT IS WHAT MATTERS

AND YOU ARE SO SMALL

YOU ARE SO SMALL AND AT BEST YOU
ARE A DISTRACTION

YOU ARE A DISTRACTION FROM WHAT
IT IS THAT I WANT

YOU ARE A DISTRACTION UNLESS YOU
ARE WHAT I HAPPEN TO WANT

YOU ARE A DISTRACTION UNLESS YOU
ARE WHAT I HAPPEN TO WANT AND
THEN YOU MATTER

YOU ARE SO SMALL AND I AM SO BIG

AND YOU MATTER YOU ONLY MATTER
YOU WILL ONLY MATTER INSOFAR AS I
WANT OR MIGHT WANT YOU

OTHER THAN THAT OTHER THAN MY
WANTING YOU YOU ARE ONLY EVER
A DISTRACTION AND HAVE NOT
MATTERED AND DO NOT MATTER AND
BEING SO SMALL YOU WILL CONTINUE
TO NOT MATTER

MACROPHILIA POEM #5

I AM BIG I AM SO BIG

I AM SO BIG AND MY VOICE IS SO LOUD

AND WHEN I SPEAK YOU CANNOT
UNDERSTAND ME BECAUSE MY VOICE
IS SO LOUD

AND INSTEAD OF UNDERSTANDING
ME YOU ONLY FEEL PAIN BECAUSE OF
THE LOUDNESS OF MY VOICE

MY VOICE IS SO LOUD THAT YOU
CANNOT EVEN HEAR IT

YOU CANNOT HEAR IT AT ALL YOU
CANNOT HEAR MY VOICE AT ALL IT CAN
ONLY HURT YOU

MACROPHILIA POEM #6

I AM BIG

I AM SO BIG

I CAN BE NEAR YOU AND NOT SEE YOU

AND WHEN I DO NOT SEE YOU IT IS BECAUSE YOU ARE SO SMALL AND I AM SO BIG

YOU ARE BENEATH ME

YOU ARE BENEATH ME AND YOU ARE BENEATH MY NOTICE

YOU ARE ALMOST NOTHING AND I AM SO BIG

YOU ARE ALMOST NOTHING AT ALL FOR SOMEONE AS BIG AS ME

THERE IS NOTHING YOU CAN DO

THERE IS NOTHING YOU CAN DO THAT I CANNOT DO AND I CAN ALWAYS DO MORE

MACROPHILIA POEM #7

I AM VERY BIG

IT IS JUST THAT I AM VERY BIG AND YOU ARE NOT

AND AS YOU ARE NOT VERY BIG THAT MAKES YOU SMALL BUT NOT JUST SMALL

THAT MAKES YOU PATHETIC YOU ARE PATHETIC

YOU ARE PATHETIC AND NOT VERY BIG

YOU ARE PATHETIC YOU ARE PATHETIC AND SMALL

YOU ARE SO SMALL

AND IT IS JUST THAT I AM VERY BIG

MACROPHILIA POEM #8

AND THEN WHAT

AND THEN I STEP ON YOU

I CRUSH YOU BY STEPPING ON YOU

asmr poem #1 asmr poem #2
asmr poem #3 asmr poem #4 by
chris sylvester

asmr poem #1: i am folding laundry for you

i am folding laundry for you

i am folding this piece of laundry for you

and i am folding this piece of laundry for you

i am telling you about folding laundry for you while i fold laundry for you

i am softly telling you about folding laundry for you while i fold all this laundry for you

and my hands are also folding laundry for you

both of my hands are also folding laundry for you

my hands are folding laundry for you while i am telling you softly about folding laundry for you this hand is folding laundry for you

and this hand is folding laundry for you

my hands are both folding laundry for you while i am softly telling you about how i am folding laundry for you and how my hands are folding laundry for you

and now i am folding this piece of laundry for you

and now i am folding this piece of laundry for you

and all the time i am folding laundry for you and this hand is

folding laundry for you and this hand is folding laundry for you and i am telling you about how i am folding laundry for you and my hands are folding laundry for you and i am folding laundry for you

asmr poem #2 a relaxing spa experience

0:00 - 15:30

0:00 hi welcome back to halo hair studio i understand you are in today for a shampoo and trim ok good i am going to ask you to just have a seat right here good ok now as you know here at halo before we begin any service we like to start with a relaxing scalp massage and that is just so that we can put you in a very calm and relaxed mood and we find that when you have achieved a state of very deep relaxation you always come away with the best results and that is what we want for all of our clients here yes so do you mind if i come a little bit closer ok good i didn't think so ok so how does that feel good that is not

too much pressure is it ok that is what i like

to hear your hair has gotten so long since the

last time i saw you yeah it really has oh my

gosh has it been that long since i've seen

you i can't believe that no i know how it is

though we just tend to get so caught up in

our busy lives that we forget to take time out

for ourselves yes it happens to the best of us

but it is always good to remember to take

time out and pamper yourself because you

are worth it no don't feel guilty it is ok be-

sides you are here now and that is what mat-

ters now i am just going to check your scalp

and make sure that everything looks healthy

ok good and on this side ok good ok ok well everything looks really great i can tell you've been taking care of yourself your hair is so shiny you are so lucky to have hair with a texture like this yes not everybody gets that my hair is kind of half way between being wavy and straight so it is just always a mess i know i do have to use a lot of product it can be kind of a pain how are you feeling are you starting to get relaxed good that is what we want i know it does feel so good doesn't it sometimes i wish that the scalp massage could last forever too but we do have to move on to the haircut eventually but you know we do have a full service spa and you can come in at any time we take walk ins

somebody will always be here for you yes

yes there is no need to call ahead or any-

thing we make sure that we are always well

staffed and we offer massages and facial

treatments we do makeup as well just about

anything you can think of we do but if you do

want to make an appointment that is fine

also just call ahead i am sorry about that ok

how are you doing good ok that concludes

the scalp massage so if you just sit tight i've

got to get a couple of things rearranged here

ok hold on just a moment ok now that that is

all taken care of if you would like to look

down you can see some of the tools that i

will be working with today ok bend over yes yes right there ok the first thing you will prob- ably notice is i have some candles here that is just to set the mood and get you nice and relaxed and they just create such a relaxing atmosphere and next we have scissors of course you couldn't have a haircut without scissors right and some bobby pins for styling ok some rubber bands also just for styling your hair and i have two different brushes this is the first one it is a detangling brush and this is of course what i am going to use to get any knots or anything like that out of your hair and second is my absolute favorite this is a boar bristle brush as you can see on the sides there and it is mixed in

with these plastic bristles and the purpose of

this brush is to distribute the natural oils in

your hair all the way along the hair shaft and

it just gives it the most beautiful shine and it

makes your hair so healthy and pretty look-

ing i just love it and as you can see it also

has the cushion part and that just gives it a i

don't know it just makes it so easy to brush

your hair and it just feels really nice so that

is my favorite brush and i have a spray bottle

and some shampoo conditioner and hair

spray that i'll be using with you alright so i'll

just have you look up for me again there we

go let me get your head straight ok alright

and now we can start by brushing your hair and like i said we're going to use this first the detangling brush like i said your hair is very healthy so you don't have too many knots or tangles your hair is so pretty i know i told you that but you must get so many compliments yes i'm hearing things i think it is the wind it is a very windy day outside and our salon is by a lot of trees so sometimes they rattle against the walls or the windows yes it is a strange location for a salon i guess but i don't know i just chose it because i love being close to nature and it is just kind of a relaxing escape for me oh you like it too good i am really glad to hear that 15:30

asmr poem #2 a relaxing spa experience

15:31 - 30:30

15:31 ok let me get over here and i'm just

brushing your hair out before your shampoo

just so that we can get all those tangles out

it makes washing easier ok so now i think i

am going to use the boar bristle brush and

this is really just i know we're going to be

washing the oils out of your hair in a minute

i just thought this would be a nice relaxing

experience so why not that is what today is

all about it is all about you and making you

feel good ok let me just comb through that

with my fingers your hair is so pretty it is al-

most a shame to cut it yes no but we do

need to trim these ends you do have a cou-

ple of split ends yes a trim is always a good

thing it keeps your hair healthy ok yes so i

think we are ready to start your shampoo so

just follow me back to the sink and i'll get

started ok so here we are at the sink and i'm

just going to tilt your chair back if you could

move your head yes just back good right

there against the sink ok how is that is that

comfortable for you ok good just want to

make sure it is not hurting your neck ok i am

going to get your water started i'm just going

to wet your hair ok ok now it is time to start

with the shampoo and this is a very fragrant

shampoo i just love the way it smells sorry i

am just getting some things arranged over here ok that is better ok how does that feel good i need a little bit more i'm just trying to get a really good lather here yes we really want to work all of that debris and product build up out of your hair ok now i am going to give you another scalp massage while i shampoo and that is just because i really want to work the cleanser into your scalp that is just going to help us get a better clean and that is what we want of course and that is not too rough or anything is it no ok good can you hear the little bubbles popping in the shampoo i like that sound they make a very soft gentle crinkly sound ok i think we are done with your shampoo so i am going to

turn the sink back on and get you all rinsed

up ok it is time to start with the deep

conditioning treatment not that you need it

of course but it is a nice thing to have 30:30

amsr poem #3: lamp work

i am drawing and i am drawing for you

i am drawing for you and i am telling you
about how i am drawing for you

i am telling you about how i am drawing for
you while i am drawing for you and the whole
time i am drawing for you

i am drawing one line for you and i am still
drawing one line for you and i am telling you
about how i am drawing it for you

and i am drawing one line back and forth across a piece of paper for you and i am still drawing this line on this piece of paper for you and i am drawing it without stopping be- cause i am drawing it for you and the whole time i am drawing it for you

i am telling you about how i am drawing for you and i am telling you about how i am drawing this one line for you and i am telling you about how i am drawing it for you and how i am still drawing it for you and i am telling you without mentioning what it is i am trying to draw for you and i am telling you without mentioning what it is i am drawing this line on as i am drawing it for you and all the time i am telling you about how i am drawing for you and about how i am drawing one line back and forth for you and i am not mentioning the line i am drawing for you and i am not mentioning the paper that i am drawing on as i am drawing for you and all the time i am still drawing for you and all the time i am still telling you about how i am drawing for you and how i am still drawing for you and all the time i am still not telling you about what i am drawing on as i am drawing for you and i am still not telling you

what i am drawing or trying to draw for you as i am drawing for you and there is a lamp in the room all the time there is a lamp in the room and there is a lamp in your room and there is a lamp in my room

asmr poem #4: asmr binaural mic test part two

[asmr binaural mic test part two]

BOOK ABT FANTASY BY CHRIS SYLVESTER PART TWO: 11 PT. FONT

poem abt money and visualizing money by chris sylvester

introduction to part one: money and
places with money

the secret is a book first published in 2006 which is important. the secret contains the secret to making money acquiring wealth and becoming happy. the secret of the book the secret is that making money acquiring wealth and becoming happy are the same thing. the secret is that to become wealthy or happy we must visualize wealth and happiness. the secret is to visualize money and you will have money and the secret to visualizing money is to not imagine or think about money but to look at money. looking at money is the best way to visualize money. this is also true and also a part of the secret. the best way to look at money is on youtube as videos of money in various serene landscapes that way you are open to getting money by looking at money in all kinds of different calming ways. it is very effective.

after learning about the secret as it was explained

in the book the secret published in 2006 i began to

wonder. after reading about the secret in the book

the secret where it was revealed to me that the

power of visualization was the secret to acquiring

money and that looking at money especially on

youtube as videos of money was the best way of

visualizing money and that visualizing money made

money come to me i began to wonder. i wondered

about the secret as it was explained in the book the

secret ie: looking at money in order to visualize

money and attract money. i wondered would the

secret operate or work in a not-watching but still

not-imagining and not-thinking-about way. for

example: if i told you about money or wrote about

money in sentences and in various places or in

various positions would this allow you to visualize

money in a way that is not the mere elaboration of a desire for money which is not the secret but a kind of coming into the place of wealth and happiness of visualization that is the secret as it is explained in the secret without you ever having really to watch anything. more importantly would it help me attract or bring money to me without watching youtube videos which i do not really like at all. would looking at the pages with the sentences about money make me have or get or acquire more money.

i could not ask the person who discovered the secret about this because the person who discovered the secret is rhonda byrne and she is obviously too busy visualizing money by looking at all the money she has already acquired by way of money visualization. this is a most effective form of visualization. she does not need to watch youtube videos that show money in different places locations and positions and she does not need descriptions of money in different sentences about how money is in a lot of different places locations and positions because she already has a lot of money in one place or location or position where she can look at it and visualize more money to add to the money she already has. therefore it seems like a pretty good idea for me to try to describe some of the most successful money visualization youtube videos and like 'make them available' to you as a bunch of sentences or whatever without the approval or support or consent of rhonda byrne who does not care about you and does not care about me and therefore will not care if i do this for you and more importantly for me. do not attempt to imagine what is described. do not think about that at all. simply look at them or read them or listen to them as they happen to you or as they happen and try to attract money to yourself while you look at or read or listen to them just try to make money come to you and please report back if these descriptions of landscapes with money help you acquire money. if they do not help you acquire more money please do not tell me about their failure to help you acquire that money as it may ruin my own attempts at visualizing money and acquiring more money. all positive responses about money and acquiring money welcome.

[lostoppp@gmail.com]

part one: money and 35 places with money

01.1 a beautifully maintained suburban lawn.

01.2 a beautifully maintained suburban lawn that is covered in money.

02.1 a glacier surrounded by a calm sea with the sky.

02.2 the sea and the sky are the same and the glacier is a pile of money.

03.1 an ariel view of farmland and trees.

03.2 an ariel view of farmland and trees and the farmland is dotted by stacks of money.

04.1 another calm ocean scene this time at evening.

04.2 it is still evening and the ocean itself is money.

05.1 another ariel view this time of a city cut by a river with a bridge going over the river.

05.2 the city is still there and the river is still there and the bridge is still there but we cannot see them because they are blocked by a tower of money.

06.1 three pyramids against a darkening sky.

06.2 the sky is getting darker and the pyramids are made of money and they are getting closer to you.

07.1 flowers.

07.2 the flowers are all money.

08.1 a field of flowers.

08.2 there are three big pyramids of money that are stacked in the field of flowers.

09.1 a slightly choppy sea that is not calm but still calming to look at.

09.2 two piles of money floating on top of a slightly choppy sea and it is still calming to look at.

10.1 the ocean again at evening.

10.2 it is still evening and a tower of money is coming up from under the ocean.

11.1 money is close to you.

11.2 money is coming closer to you.

12.1 a field of grass.

12.2 the grass was always just money.

13.1 jupiter with two comets on either side of it.

13.2 jupiter is still there and there are still two comets on either side of it but now jupiter is slowly becoming money until it is all money.

14.1 another city.

14.2 the city is obscured by more stacks of money.

15.1 money that is spread like fans of money against a black background.

15.2 the black background becomes money so that the fans of money are sitting on top of more money.

16.1 infinite expanses of money.

16.2 more and more money is being added.

17.1 stars in a night sky without clouds.

17.2 the stars are not blocked by clouds
instead they are blocked by spheres made
of money.

18.1 stacks of money against a beige background.

18.2 the beige background slowly fades to
black but the stacks of money stay where they are.

19.1 different views of seemingly endless
amounts of money.

19.2 more views of seemingly endless amounts
of money.

20.1 money that is moving away.

20.2 the money stops moving away and starts
moving closer.

21.1 a hotel lobby that is full of money.

21.2 a hotel lobby that is full of money that is
fading into more money.

22.1 unstable stacks of money.

22.2 the unstable stacks of money hold together
as stacks of money.

23.1 there is another city.

23.2 in front of this city there are pyramids
made of money.

24.1 money that is kept in order.

24.2 money that is all messy.

25.1 a road through the woods.

25.2 a road through the woods that is lined
by stacks of money.

26.1 steps made of money.

26.2 the steps made of money are placed on
the surface of the ocean and ascend toward the
sky above the ocean.

27.1 coastal rocks.

27.2 coastal rocks that are papered with money.

28.1 a body of water that becomes a field of
flowers.

28.2 on top of the field of flowers where the body
of water was there is an uneven arrangement
of money.

29.1 a peaceful garden.

29.2 the peaceful garden goes away and there is money.

30.1 the ocean again.

30.2 the ocean becomes money.

31.1 some daisies.

31.2 money.

32.1 purple money.

32.2 the money is still purple.

33.1 a harbor with boats in the harbor and a
building beside the harbor.

33.2 the harbor and the boats in the harbor
and the building beside the harbor are shadowed
by a tower of money.

34.1 a town and the land surrounding the town.

34.2 the town and the land surrounding the town
are blotted out by a stack of money several
miles high. it is actually two stacks of money. it is
actually three stacks of money. it is actually
four stacks of money. and each of the stacks
of money is several miles high.

35.1 it is jupiter again and there is still a comet
on one side of it and a comet on the other side
of it

35.2 jupiter is still made of money but the
comets are not made of money and they have
never been made of money.

part two: a very good and effective song about money and about acquiring money

i am a magnet to money i now have more than i need i am a magnet to money money money loves me i am a magnet to money i now have more than i need i am a magnet to money money money loves me i am a magnet to money i now have more than i need i am a magnet to money money money loves me i am a magnet to money i now have more than i need i am a magnet to money money money loves me i am a magnet to money oh i am a magnet to money i now have more than i need i am a magnet to money money money loves me i am a magnet to money i now have more than i need i am a magnet to money money money loves me i am a magnet to money i now have more than i need i am a magnet to money money money loves me i am a magnet to money i now have more than i need i am a magnet to money money money loves me alright now what i want you to do is put your name after money money loves me sing out your name everybody i want to hear you here we go i am a magnet to money i now have more than i need i am a magnet to money money money loves your name i am a magnet to money i now have more than i need i am a magnet to money money money loves your name that's right i am a magnet to money i now have more than i need i am a magnet to money money money loves me money money loves me money money loves me money money loves me money money loves me money money loves me money money loves me money money loves me money money loves me

conclusion to: poem about money and visualizing money

i'd like you to remember something very important. it is very important that you remember the fact that you do not serve money. you are not a servant to money. money serves you. money is your servant. money is a type of energy and it serves you. money is an energy that you can control. money is simply an energy that allows you to be free. money is your servant and money is an energy that allows you to be free. money gives you the freedom to live out your dreams. so don't scare money away by saying there isn't enough money. speak to your money. speak to your money and enjoy your money. if you speak to your money and enjoy your money you will find that money will love to be around you. money will love to be around you which means that money will not be able to resist you. money will not be able to resist you and it will multiply. money will come to you and money will multiply all around you. you will be a magnet to money and it will come to you and multiply all around you. so say right now money loves me. say right now money loves me and money is my obedient servant. say it again. say that money loves me and money is my obedient servant. enjoy money. enjoy it.

4 POEMS ABT HORSES BY CHRIS SYLVESTER

POEM THAT IS BEFORE 'POEM THAT IS 7 ARRANGEMENTS'

EACH ARRANGEMENT AS AN ARRANGEMENT IN EVERY CIRCUMSTANCE AND ALSO THESE ARRANGEMENTS GIVEN THAT THEY ARE ARRANGEMENTS AND CIRCUMSTANCES BEING WHAT THEY ARE DEPEND UPON OR ARE DEPENDENT UPON AS ARRANGEMENTS THE FACT THAT SOMEWHERE ELSE IT IS GETTING WORSE OR SOMEWHERE ELSE IT IS WORSENING AND WHERE THERE IS WORSENING GIVEN THAT THERE IS ALWAYS SOMEWHERE ELSE GETTING WORSE THERE IS A PAIR OF HORSES WHO ARE FIGHTING

GIVEN THAT ARRANGEMENTS OCCUR OR ARE
OCCURRING EVERYWHERE AND ALL OF THE TIME
THAT IS IN EVERY CIRCUMSTANCE OR
SITUATION OR OCCASION OR AS EVERY
CIRCUMSTANCE OR SITUATION OR OCCASION
IT IS ALSO THE CASE THAT SOME 'SOMEWHERE
ELSE' AS AN ARRANGEMENT THAT IS
SOMEWHERE OTHER THAN ANY GIVEN
ARRANGEMENT IS ALWAYS GETTING WORSE OR
WORSENING BECAUSE OF THAT GIVEN
ARRANGEMENT OR THAT THIS 'SOMEWHERE
ELSE' AS ANOTHER ARRANGEMENT WHICH IS
ALSO ANOTHER CIRCUMSTANCE OR SITUATION
OR OCCASION IS ALWAYS GETTING WORSE OR
WORSENING BECAUSE OF AN ARRANGEMENT
OTHER THAN ITSELF AND THIS MEANS THAT
EVERYTHING THAT HAPPENS OR IS HAPPENING
MAKES EVERYTHING ELSE WORSE ALL OF THE
TIME AND WHAT THIS ALSO MEANS IS GIVEN
THAT THERE IS ALWAYS A PAIR OF HORSES
FIGHTING WHEREVER IT IS GETTING WORSE OR

WHEREVER IT IS WORSENING AND SINCE
EVERYTHING AND EVERYWHERE IS GETTING
WORSE OR WORSENING ALL THE TIME BECAUSE
OF EVERYTHING ELSE THEN THERE MUST BE
PAIRS OF HORSES WHO ARE FIGHTING ALL THE
TIME EVERYWHERE AND ALWAYS

POEM THAT IS 7 ARRANGEMENTS

ARRANGEMENT #1: TWO HORSES THAT ARE FIGHTING

ARRANGEMENT #2: TWO HORSES THAT ARE FIGHTING

ARRANGEMENT #3: TWO HORSES THAT ARE FIGHTING

ARRANGEMENT #4: TWO HORSES THAT ARE FIGHTING

ARRANGEMENT #5: TWO HORSES THAT ARE FIGHTING

ARRANGEMENT #6: TWO HORSES THAT ARE FIGHTING

ARRANGEMENT #7: TWO HORSES THAT ARE FIGHTING

SPECULATIVE POEM ABT DIFFERENT PAIRS OF HORSES THAT ARE FIGHTING EACH OTHER RIGHT NOW AND ALL OF THE TIME ALL OVER THE PLACE

RIGHT NOW THERE IS A PAIR OF HORSES THAT
ARE FIGHTING EACH OTHER SOMEWHERE ON
SOME MOUNTAIN OR ON THE SIDE OF THE
MOUNTAIN LIKE ON ONE SIDE OF IT OR ON ONE
PART OF IT

RIGHT NOW THERE IS A PAIR OF HORSES THAT
ARE FIGHTING EACH OTHER ON THE SAME
MOUNTAIN AS BEFORE OR ON THE SAME SIDE
OF THE MOUNTAIN LIKE ON THE SAME SIDE OF
IT OR ON THE SAME PART OF IT AND THEY ARE
EXACTLY IN THE SAME PLACE AND IT IS
HAPPENING ALL OVER AGAIN THE SAME WAY IT
DID BEFORE BUT THIS TIME THERE ARE SOME
PEOPLE WHO ARE THERE ALSO AND THEY ARE
JUST PICKING UP SOME ROCKS OR STICKS OR
LIKE PINECONES AND LOOKING AT THEM AND
WAVING THEM AROUND OR SOMETHING AND
THEN THROWING THEM ALL OVER THE PLACE
AND JUST LEAVING THEM WHEREVER AFTER
THEY THROW THEM BECAUSE THEY ARE ALL LIKE
THOSE THINGS ARE STUPID OR MAYBE THEY ALL
JUST HATE MOUNTAINS IN GENERAL ALL THE
TIME AND EVERYTHING ON THEM OR ABOUT
THEM OR MAYBE THEY ARE JUST WALKING
AROUND ON THE MOUNTAIN JUST WALKING
AROUND WHEREVER BECAUSE THEY ARE LIKE IT

DOESN'T EVEN MATTER WHERE AM I ON THIS MOUNTAIN RIGHT NOW OR THEY ARE CLIMBING ON THINGS AROUND WHERE THEY ARE LIKE CLIMBING ON A ROCK OR A TREE OR ON SMALLER THINGS SO THAT THEY ARE JUST CRAWLING AROUND ALL OVER THE PLACE AND WHEN THEY SEE THE HORSES FIGHTING THEY ALL STOP WHATEVER THEY ARE DOING LIKE PICKING THINGS UP OR THROWING THINGS OR WALKING AROUND OR CLIMBING SOMETHING OR CRAWLING AROUND OR WHATEVER AND THEY ARE ALL LIKE LOOK AT THOSE TWO HORSES FIGHTING EACH OTHER REALLY HARD OVER THERE THEY ARE FIGHTING EACH OTHER LIKE THEY REALLY HATE EACH OTHER THEY ARE REALLY GOING AFTER EACH OTHER RIGHT NOW AND A BIRD LIKE A BIG BIRD LIKE AN OSPREY PROBABLY IS AROUND THE PLACE ON THE MOUNTAIN WHERE THE HORSES ARE FIGHTING OR NEAR BY TO THEM AND IT IS LIKE WHAT AND IT FLIES AWAY AND THERE IS A LOT OF GRAVEL

THAT IS ALL AROUND ON THE GROUND AND IT
IS GOING EVERYWHERE LIKE FLYING ALL OVER
THE PLACE BECAUSE OF THE HORSES KICKING
AROUND WITH THEIR HOOVES OR LIKE WHEN
THEY ARE SLIPPING AND THEY BUNCH UP THEIR
HAUNCHES AND THEN THEY DO OTHER THINGS

RIGHT NOW THERE IS A PAIR OF HORSES THAT ARE FIGHTING EACH OTHER IN AN AREA WHERE THERE IS HOUSES AND THEY ARE APART FROM OTHER HOUSES OR APART FROM OTHER AREAS WITH HOUSES AND MEANWHILE AT THE SAME TIME THEY ARE CLOSE TOGETHER TO THEMSELVES OR CLOSE TO EACH OTHER IN THIS ONE AREA AND THE HORSES ARE FIGHTING IN THAT AREA LIKE REALLY IN IT OR REALLY IN THERE LIKE IN THE AREA AND IT HAS TWO PARTS LIKE THE AREA HAS TWO PARTS THAT THE HOUSES ARE IN LIKE IN THAT PART OF THE AREA AND IT DOESN'T MATTER TO THE HORSES WHO DON'T CARE ABOUT ANYTHING BECAUSE THEY ARE JUST FIGHTING EACH OTHER LIKE BITING AND SWINGING AROUND THEIR HOOVES AND GOING CRAZY KICKING AT EACH OTHER SO IT DOESN'T MATTER TO THEM THAT THEY ARE FIGHTING LIKE REALLY IN THERE OR IN THAT SPECIFIC PART OF THE AREA AND THEY DON'T CARE AT ALL THAT THE TWO PARTS OF THE AREA

THAT THE HOUSES ARE IN ARE CALLED SUMMER WOODS AND SUMMER EGRETS AND THE WHOLE AREA TOGETHER LIKE SUMMER WOODS AND SUMMER EGRETS ALL TOGETHER AS AN AREA IS CALLED EGRETS AT SUMMER WOODS WHICH IS LIKE A STUPID THING THAT COULD BE HAPPENING WHERE TWO EGRETS ARE STANDING TOGETHER IN SOME WOODS AND IT IS SUMMER OR SOMETHING BUT IT IS SUPPOSED TO BE LIKE AN AREA WHERE THERE IS HOUSES WHICH IS ALSO STUPID BUT OKAY AND IT IS ALSO WHATEVER MAYBE A GOLF COURSE OR LIKE A CERTAIN DISTANCE FROM AN IMAX AND THERE ARE PEOPLE AND THEY ARE ALL EATING ICE CREAM AND POPCORN THAT THEY GOT FROM SOMEWHERE AND SUDDENLY A GUY ON A BIKE IS DRINKING SOME SORT OF LIQUID OR WHATEVER OUT OF A BOTTLE WHILE HE IS JUST SITTING THERE ON HIS BIKE LIKE NOT MOVING OR ANYTHING JUST SITTING THERE ON IT

RIGHT NOW THERE IS A PAIR OF HORSES THAT ARE FIGHTING EACH OTHER SOMEWHERE IN A GAP IN LIKE A MALL OR A DEPARTMENT STORE OR IN A STANDALONE STORE OR LIKE A STORE AT AN OUTLET OR IN WHEREVER THERE IS A GAP AT OR REALLY THEY ARE FIGHTING AT THE START OR THE END OF A VALLEY WHERE THE WATER COMES OUT OF THE VALLEY AND THEY ARE IN THE WATER OR OUT OF THE WATER WITH THEIR HOOVES AND THEIR LEGS EVEN THOUGH ALL THAT MATTERS IS THAT THEY ARE FIGHTING IN A GAP LIKE ALMOST IN OR OUT OF A VALLEY USING THEIR HOOVES AND THEIR LEGS TO FIGHT EACH OTHER WHEN THEY ARE IN THE WATER OR WHEN THEY ARE OUT OF THE WATER LIKE KICKING AT EACH OTHER LIKE REALLY GOING AFTER EACH OTHER BY KICKING AT EACH OTHER

RIGHT NOW THERE IS A PAIR OF HORSES THAT ARE FIGHTING EACH OTHER NEAR THESE TWO PEOPLE WHO DON'T KNOW THAT THERE ARE TWO HORSES FIGHTING NEAR THEM AND IF THEY DID KNOW LIKE IF THEY SAW THEM FIGHTING AND THEN THEY KNEW THAT THESE HORSES WERE FIGHTING NEAR THEM THEY WOULD PROBABLY BE ALL SCARED AND SAY SOMETHING STUPID ABOUT THE HORSES BEING SO NEAR TO THEM WHILE THEY ARE FIGHTING BECAUSE LIKE ALL OF THE OTHER PEOPLE IN THE WORLD OTHER THAN THEM THEY ARE STUPID WHEN THEY GET SURPRISED AND LIKE ALL OF THOSE OTHER PEOPLE OTHER THAN THEM THEY WILL SAY SOMETHING STUPID BECAUSE THEY GET SURPRISED LIKE IF THESE TWO PEOPLE SAW THE HORSES FIGHTING NEAR THEM THEY WOULD PROBABLY SAY SOMETHING LIKE WHOSE HORSES ARE THOSE OR I AM SCARED BY LOOKING AT THOSE HORSES OR WHAT IS THAT HORSE FIGHT ALL ABOUT OR

WHAT ARE THOSE HORSES FIGHTING FOR OR I
HAVE NEVER SEEN THOSE HORSES BEFORE OR
WHY ARE THOSE HORSES AROUND THIS PLACE
AND SO NEAR TO US

RIGHT NOW THERE IS A PAIR OF HORSES THAT ARE FIGHTING EACH OTHER AT THE CORNER OR ONE OF THE JOINTS OF A STRUCTURE LIKE WHERE TWO WALLS COME TOGETHER TO MAKE A CORNER OR A PLACE THAT STICKS OUT OF THE STRUCTURE OR AWAY FROM THE STRUCTURE OR EVEN LIKE A FEW STRUCTURES THAT ARE STANDING AROUND KIND OF CLOSE TO EACH OTHER BUT NOT TOO CLOSE TO EACH OTHER AND THERE IS A POINT OR LIKE A PLACE WHERE THEY ARE CLOSE TO EACH OTHER OR KIND OF COME TOGETHER OR WHATEVER LIKE A PLACE WHERE THEIR CORNERS ARE NEAR EACH OTHER AND WHERE THEY COME TOGETHER AND THERE IS ENOUGH ROOM WHERE TWO HORSES CAN FIGHT EACH OTHER LIKE REALLY GO TO TOWN ON EACH OTHER VERY NEAR TO THEM OR CLOSE TO THEM

RIGHT NOW THERE IS A PAIR OF HORSES THAT
ARE FIGHTING EACH OTHER IN A JUNGLE OR A
GROUP OF TREES THAT ARE CLOSE TO EACH
OTHER OR REALLY CLOSE OR CLOSE TOGETHER
IN A GROUP AND IT IS IMPORTANT THAT THEY
ARE REALLY MAKING IT HARD ON THE HORSES
WHO ARE FIGHTING EACH OTHER BECAUSE
THEIR BODIES KEEP GETTING LIKE STUCK OR
ALL WEDGED UP IN BETWEEN THE TREES AND
THE HORSES HAVE TO USE THEIR TEETH ON
EACH OTHER BECAUSE THEIR LEGS AND THEIR
BODIES ARE ALL WEDGED UP IN BETWEEN THE
TRUNKS OF THE TREES SO THAT THEY HAVE TO
STRETCH OUT THEIR NECKS AND USE THEIR
TEETH TO BITE EACH OTHER ON THE NECK OR
ON THE FACE AND THERE IS BLOOD ALL OVER
THEIR NECKS AND ALL ON THEIR FACES AND
ALSO ALL OVER THE TREES LIKE ALL OVER THE
TRUNKS OF THE TREES AND ALSO THE LEAVES

RIGHT NOW THERE IS A PAIR OF HORSES THAT ARE FIGHTING EACH OTHER AND IT IS HAPPENING AT A VERY HIGH FRAME RATE LIKE AT 48FPS OR PROBABLY LIKE EVEN HIGHER THAN THAT LIKE 64FPS OR 72FPS AND IT IS GIVING SOME PERSON WHO IS WATCHING IT A HEADACHE OR WHATEVER LIKE A FEELING OF PAIN OR CONFUSION OR ANOTHER FEELING LIKE OF A DISCOMFORT OR SOMETHING THAT IS HAPPENING WITH THE EYES LIKE THAT HAPPENS WITH THEM OR AROUND THEM AND WITH THE HEAD ALSO

RIGHT NOW THERE IS A PAIR OF HORSES THAT ARE FIGHTING EACH OTHER OVER SOME RUBIES LIKE OVER THEM OR ABOVE THEM LIKE THERE IS A CAVE THAT THEY ARE IN AND THERE ARE RUBIES IN THE CAVE JUST LIKE LYING AROUND EVERYWHERE AND THE GROUND IS ALL MUDDY IN THE CAVE AND THERE ARE RUBIES ALL IN THE MUD BECAUSE THEY WERE LYING AROUND EVERYWHERE BEFORE JUST LIKE ALL OVER THE PLACE AND NOW THE HORSES ARE STEPPING ON THEM WHILE THEY ARE FIGHTING AND THE HORSES DON'T EVEN NOTICE THEM OR REALLY LIKE THEY DON'T CARE ABOUT THE RUBIES BECAUSE THEY ARE HORSES AND BECAUSE THEY ARE GOING AT EACH OTHER LIKE REALLY GOING AFTER ONE ANOTHER AND ALSO BECAUSE IT IS SO DARK LIKE VERY DARK IN THE CAVE BUT WHEN THEY STEP ON THEM THERE IS A SOUND THAT HAPPENS OR LIKE A CLACKING THING WHICH DOESN'T MATTER BECAUSE IT IS ALL MUDDY IN THE CAVE AND

THERE IS ALL THE SUCKING OF THE MUD WHEN
THEY MOVE AROUND ON THEIR LEGS TO KICK AT
EACH OTHER WITH THEIR MUDDY HOOVES WITH
RUBIES ALL IN THE MUD STUCK TO THEIR
HOOVES AND THERE IS THE HORSE SCREAMING
AND THE HORSE FLANK ALL IN THE DARK
EVERYWHERE AND THE HORSE SWEAT

//OR// THE TWO HORSES ARE FIGHTING EACH OTHER AT THE MOUTH OF THE CAVE AND THE RUBIES ARE SPILLING OUT FROM THE MOUTH OF THE CAVE AND THEY ARE ALL OVER THE PLACE WHERE THE HORSES ARE FIGHTING BUT MAYBE IT IS NIGHT OR MAYBE IT IS DAY OR WHATEVER

HORSE QUA MECH POEM

WHAT DOES THE HORSE HANGAR LOOK LIKE HE ASKS. I DO NOT ANSWER. I DO NOT LIKE HIM AND I DO NOT KNOW WHY HE IS HERE. AND ANYWAY, IT IS BECOMING VISIBLE NOW. HE IS TOO STUPID TO NOTICE. YES. IT IS THERE: A LOW STRUCTURE ON THE FROZEN HORIZON— ROUNDED TOWARD THE TOP AND COVERED WITH ICE AND SNOW. IT SQUATS IN ITS PLACE, STAYING THE SAME SIZE AS WE MOVE OVER THE IMPASSABLE FURROWS AND CREVICES OF THE GLACIER. THE TERRAIN DOES NOT AFFECT OUR HORSE TRANSPORT IN THE LEAST. THE ICE SLIDING BELOW US IS DIRTY, YEARS OF PARTICULATE SHOWING SLATE AND DULL, AND BEYOND THAT THERE IS ONLY THE WEIRD LIGHT WITH THE SHAPE OF THE HANGAR STUCK IN IT AND THE SOUND OF STEAM LEAVING THE HORSE'S FLANK VENTS. MY GOD HE SAYS BESIDE ME JUST NOW NOTICING IT AND I TURN WITHOUT RESPONDING AND LEAVE THE DECK, ENTERING THE WARM INSIDES OF THE HORSE.

WITHIN AN HOUR WE DOCK—THE TRANSPORT ROCKING INTO ITS SLIP WITH A WHICKER, THE GIANT DOORS OF THE HORSE HANGAR SHUTTING SLOWLY, A VIBRATING IN THE DISTANCE. COMING OUT ONTO THE DECK I AM STRUCK BY THE SIGHT AND HE, COMING UP BEHIND ME, SAYS OH GOD AGAIN. THIS IS WHAT WE SEE: ROW UPON ROW OF HORSES, OF A VARIETY OF MAKES AND MODELS, ALL SUSPENDED OFF THE GROUND BY THEIR SUPPORT TRUSSES AND COMPLEX SCAFFOLDS, THEIR REFUELING LINES, SOME DRAPING LIKE STREAMERS, SAGGING AWAY FROM THE HORSES' BODIES, DIPPING LOW AND THEN ASCENDING TOWARD THEIR SEPARATE POINTS OF CONNECTION WITH THE CEILING, SOME SHOOTING STRAIGHT OUT OF THE SHADOWS AND RECESSES OF THE HORSE HANGAR IN THE NEAR OR FAR DISTANCE TO DOCK WITH ONE HORSE OR ANOTHER AT VARIOUS POINTS ACROSS ITS FLANK OR SOMEWHERE ON ITS

UNDERCARRIAGE, OR AT THE HAUNCHES, OR UP AND DOWN A SET OF LEGS, OR UNDER ITS CHIN, OR BY WAY OF THE MOUTH AND DOWN THE THROAT, OR IN THE TANGLES OF ITS MANE AND CONTINUING ALONG THE SPINE.

THE HORSES THEMSELVES ARE MASSIVE. EASILY TEN TIMES THE SIZE OF OUR TRANSPORT, THOUGH THE UNUSUAL SPACES OF THE HORSE HANGAR ITSELF TEND TO MAKE EACH EYE A HORSE OF ITS OWN AS THEY SAY HERE. ONE HORSE IS CREWED BY AT LEAST 50 HUMANS OR NEAR-HUMAN PONY-BLENDS: PILOTS, NAVIGATORS, MECHANICS, ARTILLERYMEN, AND EQUINE ENGINEERS OR SADDLERS, EVERY ONE OF THEM ESSENTIAL TO THE OPERATION OF THE HORSE AND NONE OF THEM IN EVIDENCE NOW. SOMEWHERE I KNOW THEY ARE EATING IN A SLOP HOUSE OR MEAT SCRAPE OR SHOWERING ALL TOGETHER WHILE HOLDING VARIOUS POSES FOR LONG PERIODS LIKE THEY ARE KNOWN TO DO. THOUGH MOST LIKELY, WHEREVER THEY ARE, THEY ARE DOING THINGS TO OTHER THINGS WITH THEIR HANDS. EVEN IN THEIR ABSENCE THE HORSE HANGAR IS FILLED WITH ACTIVITY. SMALL FIGURES OF MEN AND WOMEN MOVE WITH SURENESS AND PRECISION

ABOUT THE NETWORK OF TIGHT WALKWAYS ERECTED UPON THE SCAFFOLDING AROUND EACH HORSE. I KNOW WHO THEY ARE. THEY ARE THE TAIL GREASERS, THE HOOF SUCKS, THE WASH BOYS AND THE MANE GIRLS, THOSE WHO CRAWL AROUND ON THE SKIN OF HORSES AND NEVER SEE THEIR INSIDES, WHO ARE CALLED AND CALL THEMSELVES LICE AND WHO DIE DOZENS AT A TIME EVERY DAY WITH THE FLICK OF A TAIL OR A LAZY BUT UNEXPECTED KICK OR THE SUDDEN DISCHARGE OF A HORSE LASER BEING WELDED AND POLISHED BY A CREW OF TWENTY OR MORE. THEY DO NOT CARE ABOUT THEIR LIVES AND IN ANY CASE THERE ARE ALWAYS MORE TO TAKE THEIR PLACE. THE FLESH OF THE HORSE IS THE EXTENT OF THEIR WORLD AND THE EXTENT OF THEIR CONCERNS.

THE SOUNDS OF THE WORK BEING DONE WOULD BE OVERWHELMING, BUT THE DISTANCE FROM THE HORSES THEMSELVES AS WELL AS THE HIGH CEILINGS AND GENERAL HUGENESS OF THE HANGAR SEEM TO MUTE THE ROAR OF CUTTING, WELDING, SHOUTING ALONG WITH THE SOUNDS OF A WHOLE HOST OF OTHER OPERATIONS TAKING PLACE AROUND AND UPON THE BODIES OF THE HORSES. ONE NEAR THE CENTER OF THE HANGAR FLEXES ITS LEGS METHODICALLY EACH AFTER THE OTHER WHILE A MASSIVE ROBOTIC CLAW GENTLY INSERTS HEAT-SEEKING MISSILES INTO THEIR CHASSIS, WHICH ARE ANCHORED IN THE HORSE'S BACK NEAR A SATELLITE DISH THAT EVEN NOW ROTATES THOUGH THE HORSE IS ONLY PARTIALLY OPERATIONAL, IN THAT NON-BATTLE STATE WHICH DIFFERS ALMOST ENTIRELY FROM THE APPEARANCE OR IMAGE WE ARE ALL SO FAMILIAR WITH, WHICH EVEN A CHILD COULD DRAW FROM MEMORY: THE HORSE

AFTER THE ASSUMPTION OF ITS FINAL AND HORRIFYING FORM.

ALL AROUND US HANG OTHER HORSES SMALLER OR LARGER THAN THAT ONE, GLEAMING WITH THE CARE AND ATTENTION GIVEN ONLY TO MACHINES OF DEATH; EVEN THE SCARS OF FORMER BATTLES SEEMING TO SHINE WITH A HIGH POLISH. ALONG THEIR FLANKS ARE PAINTED NAMES FAMILIAR OR UNFAMILIAR, SOME OF WHOM EVEN YOU MAY RECOGNIZE. AS A SALUTE AND A SUPPLICATION, I PROVIDE HEREAFTER A DESCRIPTION OF JUST THOSE HORSES, COMMON TO OUR POPULAR KNOWLEDGE, REVERED, RESPECTED, AND DREADED FOR THEIR TERRIBLE AND GLORIOUS, THEIR BLOODED DEEDS:

THERE IS THE HORSE CALLED BLACK DRAGON PILOTED BY NECRON WITH ITS MACHINE GUNS HANGING AT REST FROM ITS FLANKS, THE ROUNDED HEADS OF THE SMALL MISSILES NESTED IN THE HORSE'S CHEST, PIMPLE-LIKE, SHINING IN THE FLAT LIGHT OF THE HORSE HANGAR, ITS DEADLY HOOF MOUNTED GRENADE LAUNCHERS LOOKING SLIGHTLY RIDICULOUS WHEN LIMPLY NOT IN USE.

THERE IS THE HORSE CALLED SCORPION 5.0 PILOTED BY MILLICONA WHOSE LASER CANNONS, PULSE CANNONS, AND SLUG GUNS SWING BACK AND FORTH, DECISIVELY, FIRST ONE BY ONE, AND THEN ALL AT ONCE, AND THEN AGAIN IN VARIOUS COMBINATIONS, UNDERGOING A SYSTEMS CHECK MORE THAN LIKELY, AS A GROUP OF LICE GO ABOUT SOME INDETERMINATE WORK UPON THE HORSE'S NECK.

THERE IS THE HORSE CALLED PALE HORSE PILOTED BY DARK RIDER: ITS DUAL GRENADE LAUNCHERS (ONE MOUNTED ON EACH SIDE OF THE HORSE'S HAUNCHES) ARE ALSO BEING TESTED, SWIVELING BACK AND FORTH TO FOLLOW THE TARGETING RETICULE ISSUED BY ITS TONGUE MOUNTED LASER CANNON.

THERE IS THE HORSE CALLED STEEL DRAGON PILOTED BY TIAMAT WHOSE MULTI-MISSILE SYSTEM IS ALSO CAPABLE OF LAUNCHING AND DIRECTING SWARMS OF FLESH-STRIPPING DRONES OR 'HORSE-FLIES' AND WHOSE TERRIFYING FACE BAZOOKA IS ONLY WHISPERED OR MUTTERED ABOUT, AND ONLY IF IT MUST BE MENTIONED.

THERE IS THE HORSE CALLED PANZERN VII PILOTED BY RAVE WHOSE LASER CANNONS, BIO-INTEGRATED INTO THE HORSE ITSELF, ARE WIELDED WITH HORRIBLE PRECISION, AND WHOSE MACHINE GUNS ARE FITTED JUST ABOVE ITS EARS, WHILE ITS GRENADE LAUNCHER APPEARS FROM BEHIND A PANEL IN ITS CHEST, WHICH IS REPEATEDLY BEING OPENED AND CLOSED TO ADJUST ITS TIMING AND INCREASE EFFICIENCY.

THERE IS THE HORSE CALLED DARK NIGHT PILOTED BY SHADOW, A HORSE OF RELATIVELY SMALL STATURE, THOUGH OUTFITTED WITH A PLASMA RIFLE THAT IS DEADLY AT HUGE, AND OFFICIALLY UNDISCLOSED, DISTANCES, AND WHOSE DUAL MISSILE TECHNOLOGY IS RARELY NEEDED TO DOUBLE TAP A TARGET OR FINISH THE JOB.

THERE IS THE HORSE CALLED SCORPION 4.0 PILOTED BY ENTITY, ITS HUGE BULK DOMINATED BY THE ROCKET LAUNCHER GRAFTED TO ITS BACK, THOUGH THE REAL DANGER OF THIS HORSE IS ITS MATCHING, FRONT AND BACK LEG-MOUNTED, MACHINE GUNS, OR "CUTTERS," AND THE GRENADE LAUNCHER NESTED BENEATH ITS TAIL, WHICH COVERS ITS REAR.

THERE IS THE HORSE CALLED RED DRAGON PILOTED BY LORD SLAYER THAT WAS FIVE YEARS RETIRED, GONE TO THE ICE PASTURE, BUT RECENTLY FOUND ITS WAY OUT OF DEEP FREEZE TO BE REFITTED WITH A NEW 16-CHAMBER META-HEART, A MESH-FLESH HYBRID BLADDER (WHICH BOTH PROCESSES AND REINTEGRATES URINE AND PRECISELY REGULATES BUOYANCY FOR AMPHIBIOUS MANEUVERS), AND A SINGLE, PSEUDO-CHAMBERED, ENTIRELY COLLAPSIBLE AND GILL-ENABLED, LUNG-SACK, NOT TO MENTION THE STATE OF THE ART PLASMA RIFLE CAPABLE OF RENDERING HORSEFLESH INTO A KIND OF MOLTEN SLAG ON CONTACT, AS WELL AS THE HIGH-CALIBER SLUG GUN OF THE SAME MODEL MOUNTED ON THE HORSE SCORPION 5.0.

THERE IS THE HORSE CALLED PANZERN VI WHOSE PILOT TIGER IS RENOWNED FOR HIS PROWESS WITH A SPECIALLY DESIGNED, NEURALLY INTERFACING, MULTI-MISSILE SYSTEM, THE LAUNCHING PORTS OF WHICH ARE DISTRIBUTED ACROSS HIS HORSE'S BODY— SAVE FOR ITS BACK RIGHT LEG THAT, IN ITS ENTIRETY, CONVERTS TO A BAZOOKA ON COMMAND, BECOMING A POTENT WEAPON AT THE COST OF AN AWKWARD MODIFICATION, A JOKE THAT HAS NOT BEEN LOST ON THE OTHER CREWS, WHICH CALL THE HORSE 'CRIPPLE.'

FINALLY: THERE IS THE HORSE CALLED SCORPION 3.0 PILOTED BY DEMISE, CURRENTLY HANGING UPSIDE DOWN IN ORDER TO EXPOSE ITS UNDERCARRIAGE TO AN AUTOMATED WASHING PROCESS ACCOMPLISHED BY MULTIPLE ROBOTIC LIMBS DESCENDING FROM THE CEILING OF THE HORSE HANGAR, THOUGH EACH OF THESE LIMBS IS ALSO RIDDEN BY A HORDE OF LICE NO DOUBT INTENT ON CAREFULLY GUIDING THE OPERATION AND WHO ARE MET BY STILL MORE WAITING ON THE HORSE ITSELF, EACH OF THEM IN THEIR STUPID DEVOTION DO NOT SEEM TO NOTICE THEIR CLOSENESS TO OR REMEMBER THE STATISTICAL LIKELIHOOD OF THEIR DEATH AND EVEN NOW, EVEN AT THIS MOMENT, PAY NO MIND AS ONE OF THEIR COHORT SLIDES OFF THE STOMACH OF THE HORSE, WASHED OVER BY THE HIGH PINK SCRUM OF PRESSURIZED DISINFECTANT FLUID, DROPPING PAST THE WHOLE STORIED ARSENAL OF THIS LETHAL AND HOOVED ANGEL,

AN ARESENAL THAT STILL THREATENS IN ITS NON-OPERATIONAL SLACKNESS: PAST ITS FLANK-MOUNTED LASER CANNONS, PAST ITS DUAL PURPOSE BACK-CANNON/BAZOOKA, BEFORE GETTING LOST IN THE STREAMS OF WATER AND CHEMICAL FOAM DRIPPING OFF THE HORSE, DISAPPEARING FROM VIEW LONG BEFORE MEETING THE HANGAR FLOOR, ALL WITHOUT THE SLIGHTEST SOUND, OR AT LEAST A SOUND THAT COULD BE HEARD AT THIS DISTANCE.

OF COURSE, AS WE ALL KNOW AND AS THE LICE KNOW BEST OF ALL DEATH IS NO REASON OR CAUSE FOR SADNESS OR PITY OR DESPAIR. TO DIE HERE IN THE HORSE HANGAR IS TO BLESS THEIR STABLE AND MARK THEIR GATE AND FURTHER IT IS TO PARTICIPATE IN THE ENDLESS DRESSAGE OF THE FULLY BRIDLED AND THE FULLY BLOODED. LET THEIR NAMES MEAN NOTHING BUT DEATH WHEN SPOKEN AND LET THE EARTH BE POISONED WHEREVER THEY SHOULD RIDE.

ROOF BOOKS
the best in language since 1976

Recent & Selected Titles

· IN THE FACE OF by David Buuck. 104 p. $16.95
· FRANKLINSTEIN by Susan Landers. 144 p. $16.95
· PLATO'S CLOSET by Lawrence Giffin. 144 p. $16.95
· we plié by Patrick R. Phillips. 120 p. $16.95
· social patience by David Brazil. 136 p. $15.95
· PARSIVAL by Steve McCaffery. 88 p. $15.95
· THE PHOTOGRAPHER by Ariel Goldberg. 84 p. $15.95
· TOP 40 by Brandon Brown. 138 p. $15.95
· DEAD LETTER by Jocelyn Saidenberg. 98 p. $15.95
· THE MEDEAD by Fiona Templeton. 314 p. $19.95
· LYRIC SEXOLOGY VOL. 1 by Trish Salah. 138 p. $15.95
· INSTANT CLASSIC by erica kaufman 90 p. $14.95
· A MAMMAL OF STYLE by Kit Robinson
& Ted Greenwald. 96 p. $14.95
· VILE LILT by Nada Gordon. 114 p. $14.95
· DEAR ALL by Michael Gottlieb. 94 p. $14.95
· FLOWERING MALL by Brandon Brown. 112 p. $14.95.
· MOTES by Craig Dworkin. 88 p. $14.95
· APOCALYPSO by Evelyn Reilly. 112 p. $14.95
· BOTH POEMS by Anne Tardos. 112 p. $14.95

Roof Books are published by
Segue Foundation
300 Bowery · New York, NY 10012
For a complete list, please visit **roofbooks.com**

Roof Books are distributed by
SMALL PRESS DISTRIBUTION
1341 Seventh Street · Berkeley, CA. 94710-1403.
spdbooks.org